FAIRIES

Line Art Coloring Book
by Christine Karron

Recommended for coloring with colored pencils,
markers, pens and/or crayons.
If using wet media place a sheet of thick paper or card
behind the coloring page to prevent bleed through.

All illustrations in this coloring book were originally created and
completely traditionally hand drawn by the artist Christine Karron.
Please visit www.chkarron.com for more about Christine's artwork.

No part of this book may be reproduced or transmitted in any form or by any
means, electronic or mechanical, including photocopying, recording or by any
information storage and retrieval system, without written permission from the
copyright holder, except for a book review.

Fairies
Line Art Coloring book by Christine Karron
First published June 2018

ISBN-13: 978-1722294380
ISBN-10: 1722294388

Copyright 2018 Christine Karron
All rights reserved.

www.chkarron.com

FAIRIES

1. Dragonfly Fairy
2. Pine Tree Fairy
3. Calla Lily Fairy
4. Rowan tree Fairy
5. Water Lily Fairy
6. Forget Me Not Fairy
7. River Fairy
8. Blueberry Fairy
9. Daisy Fairy
10. Butterfly Fairy
11. Bleeding Hearts Fairy
12. Firefly Fairy
13. Fern Fairy
14. Lily Of The Valley Fairy
15. Dandelion Fairy
16. Birdsong Fairy
17. Cattail Fairy
18. Oak Tree Fairy
19. Snow Fairy
20. North Wind Fairy

Bonus

21. Dancing Mouse Couple
22. Mother Goose
23. Robin Christmas
24. Dandelion Fairy (grayscale)

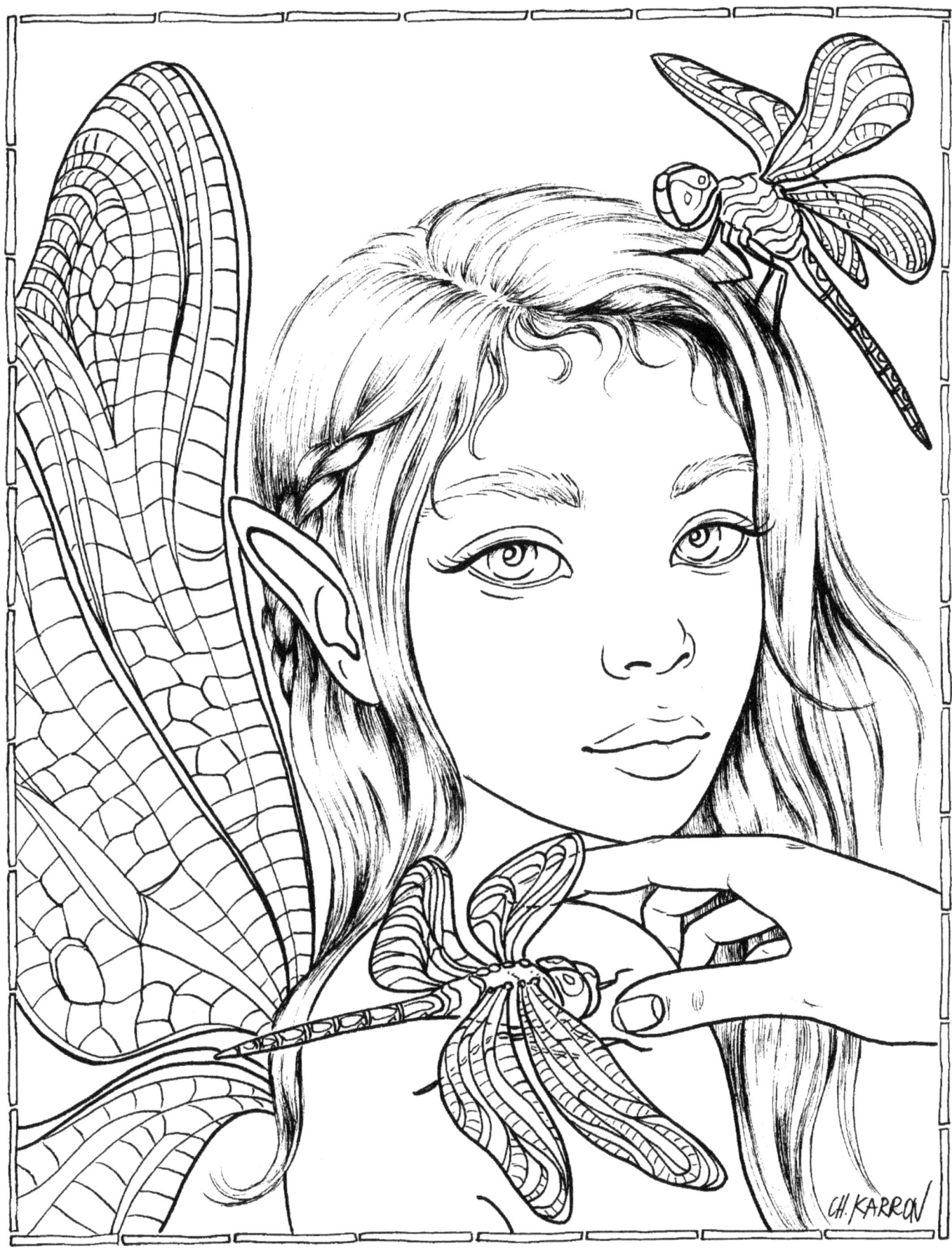

Fairies by Christine Karron

Dragonfly Fairy

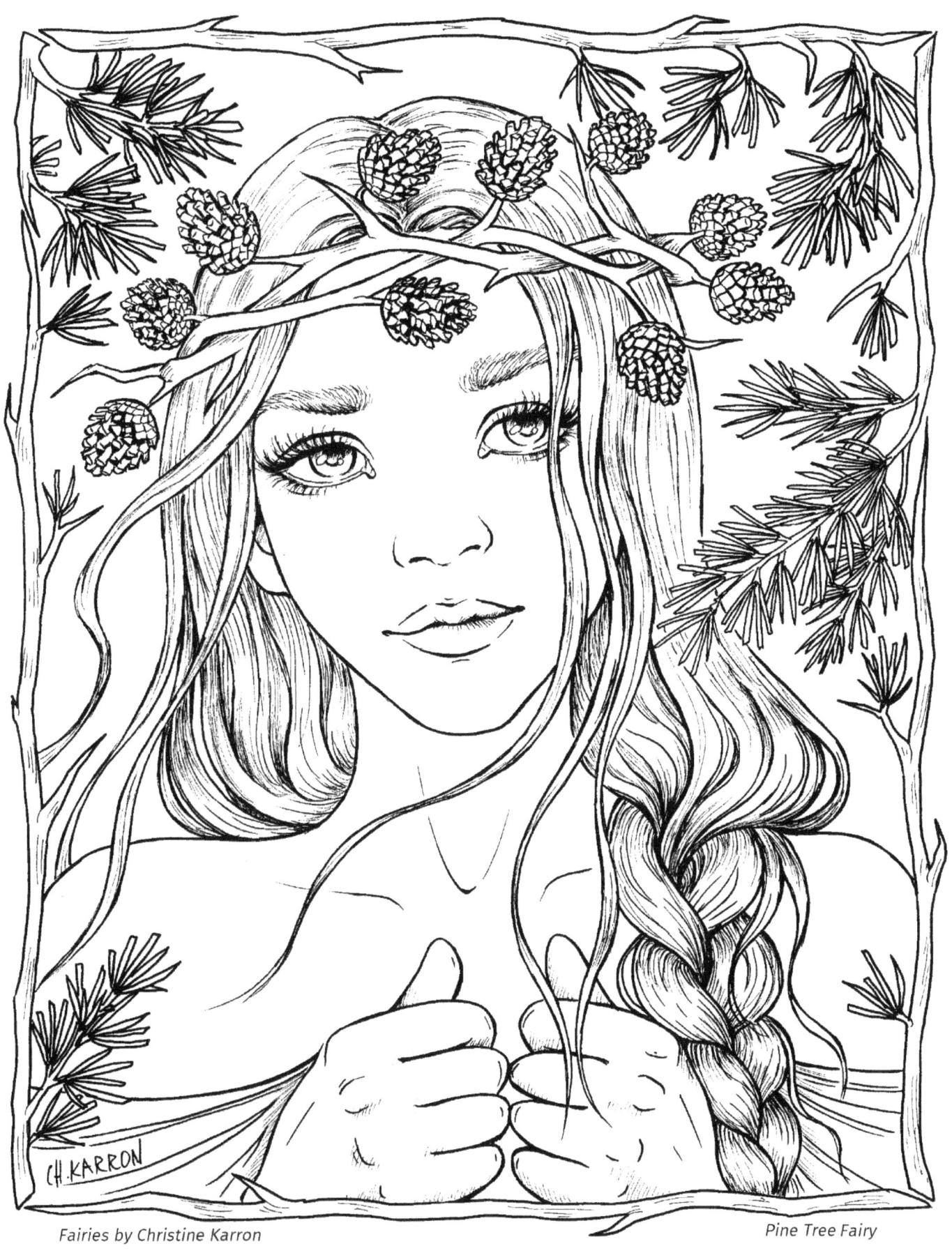

Fairies by Christine Karron — Pine Tree Fairy

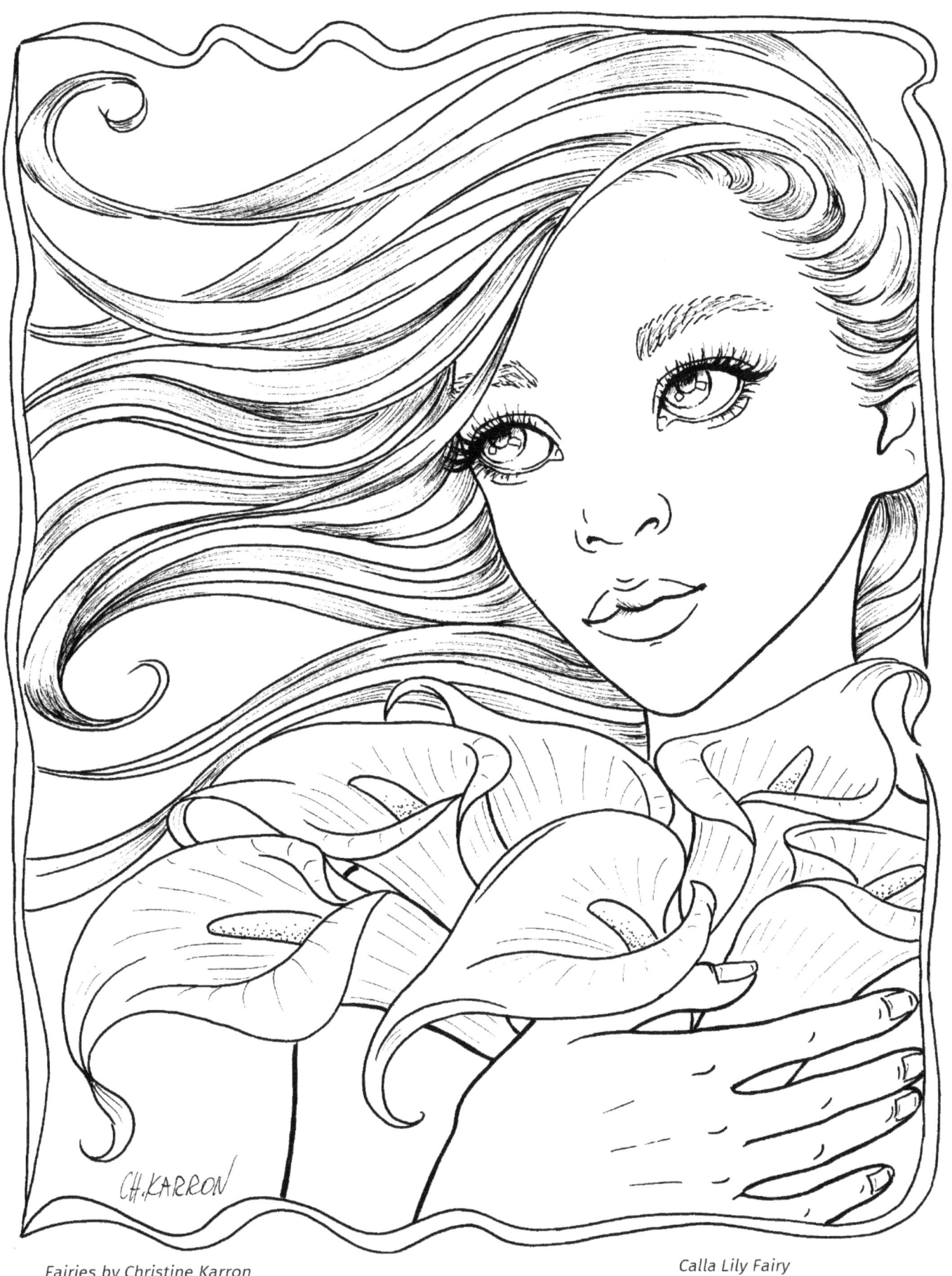

Fairies by Christine Karron

Calla Lily Fairy

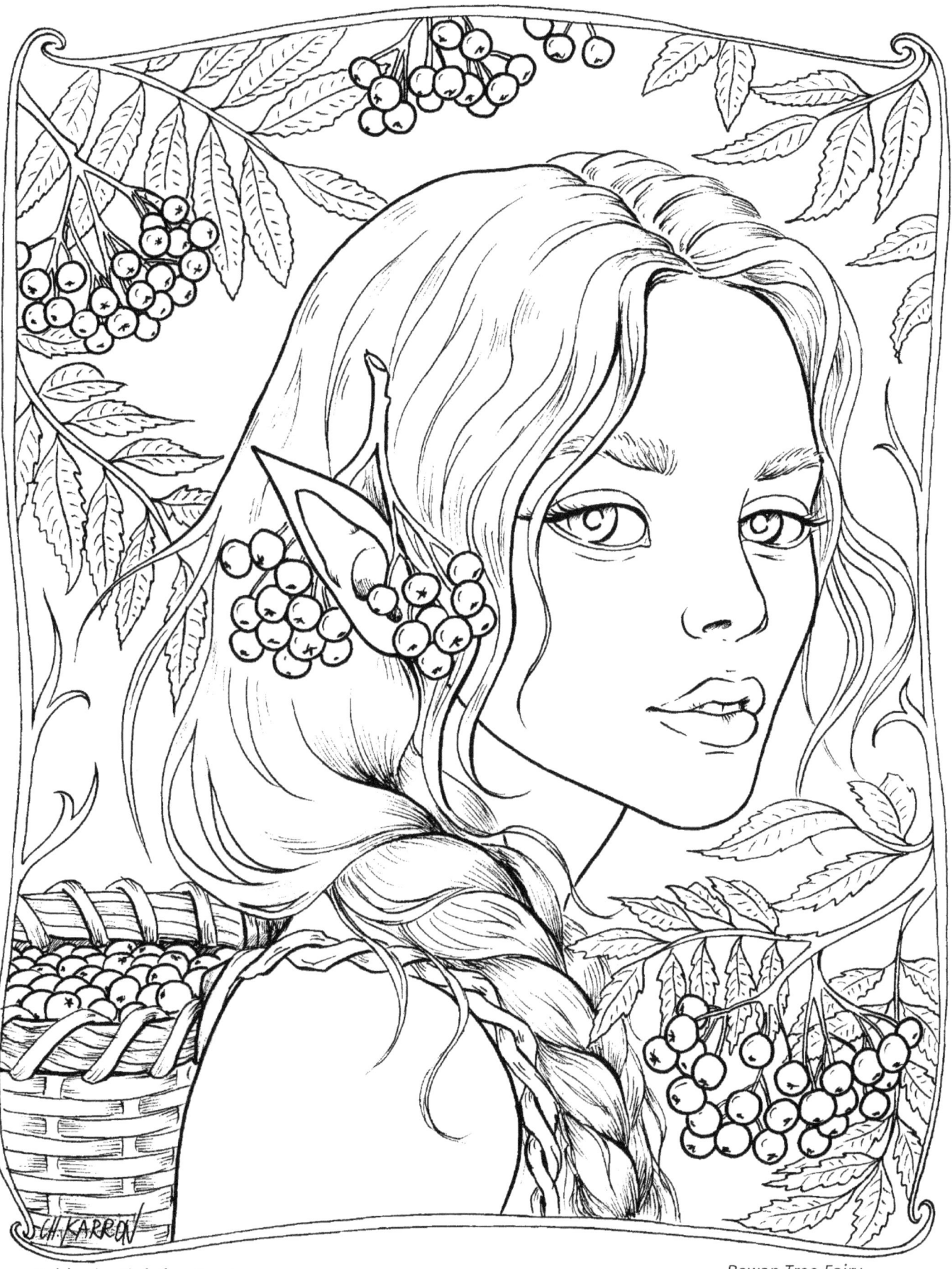

Fairies by Christine Karron

Rowan Tree Fairy

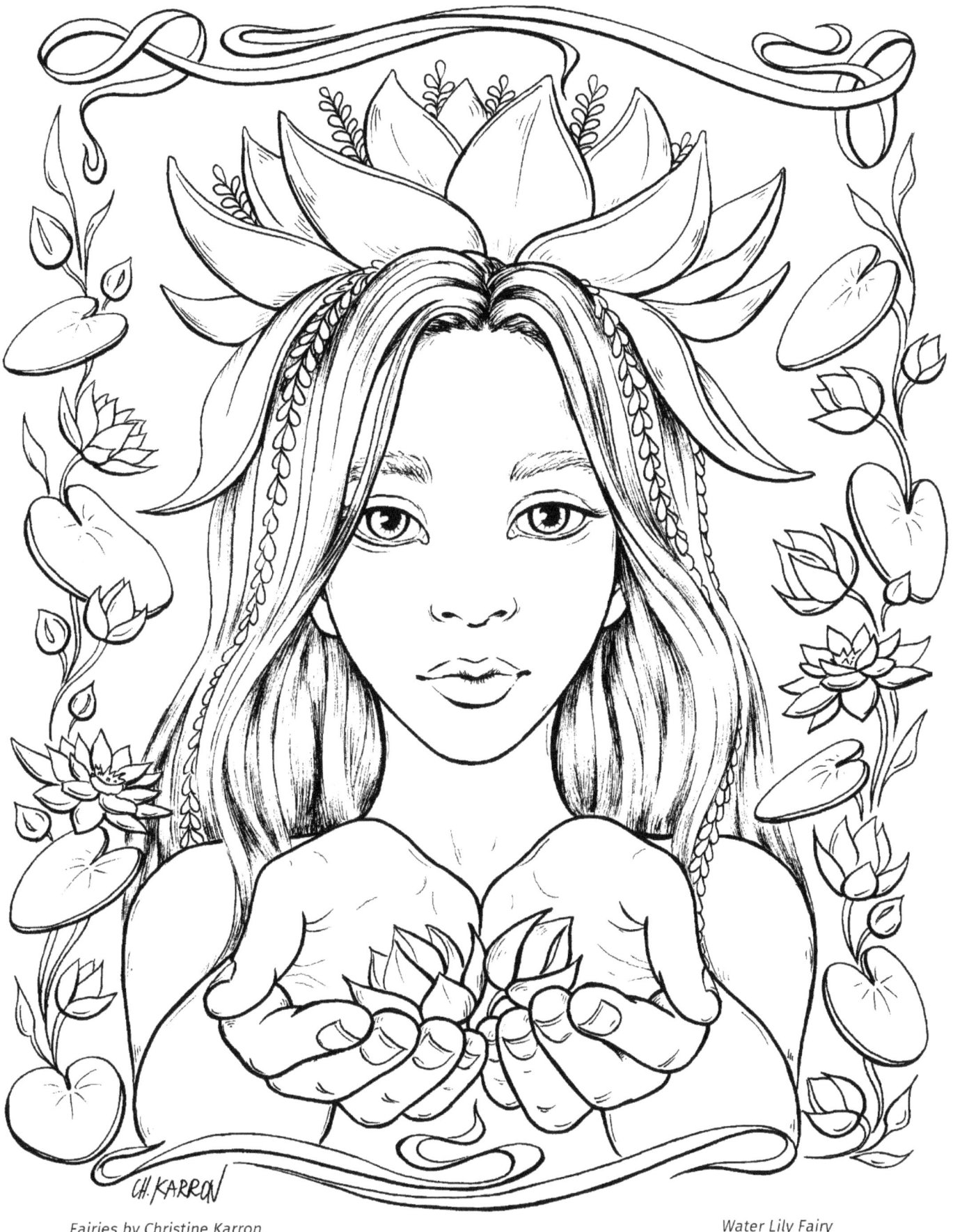

Fairies by Christine Karron

Water Lily Fairy

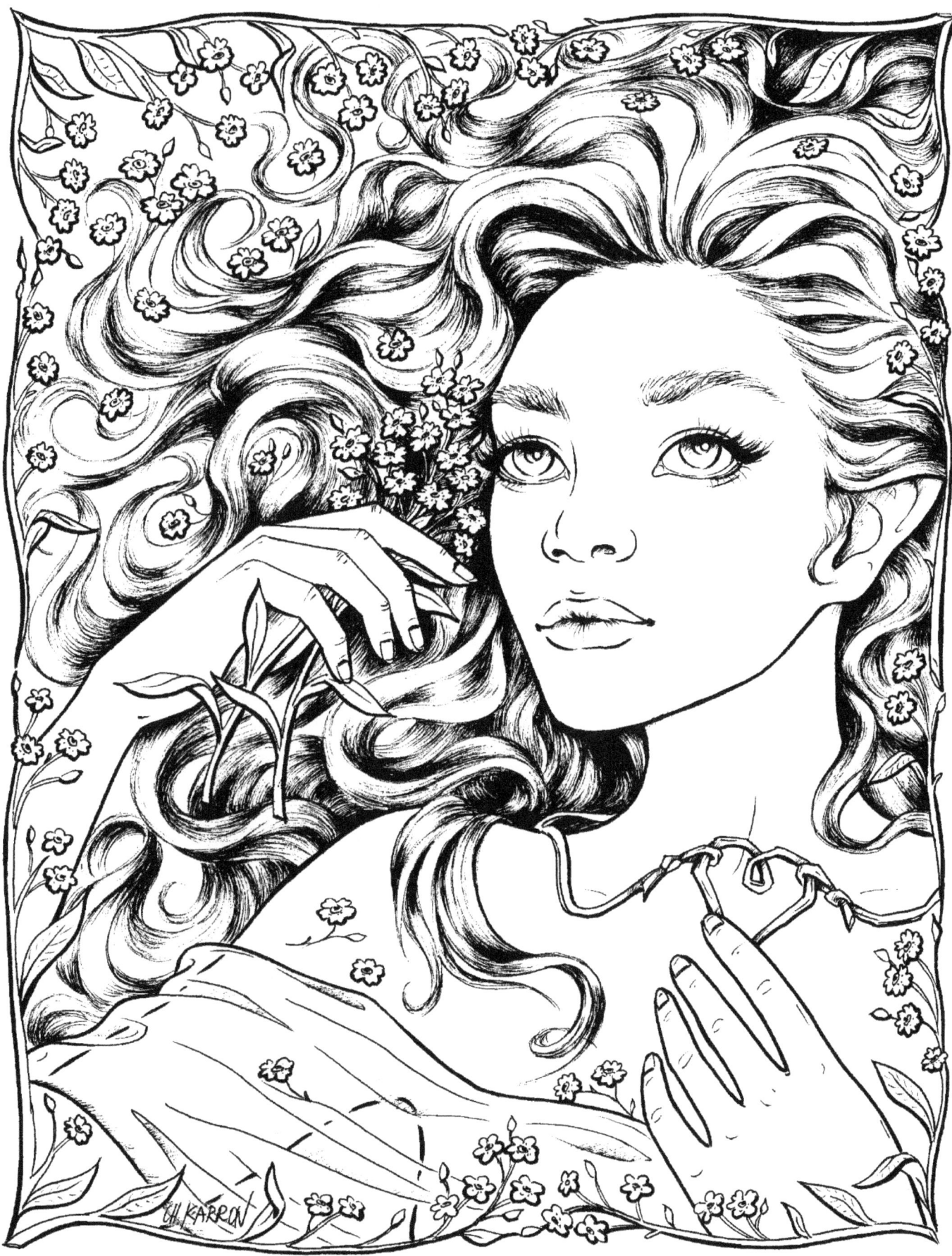

Fairies by Christine Karron

Forget Me Not Fairy

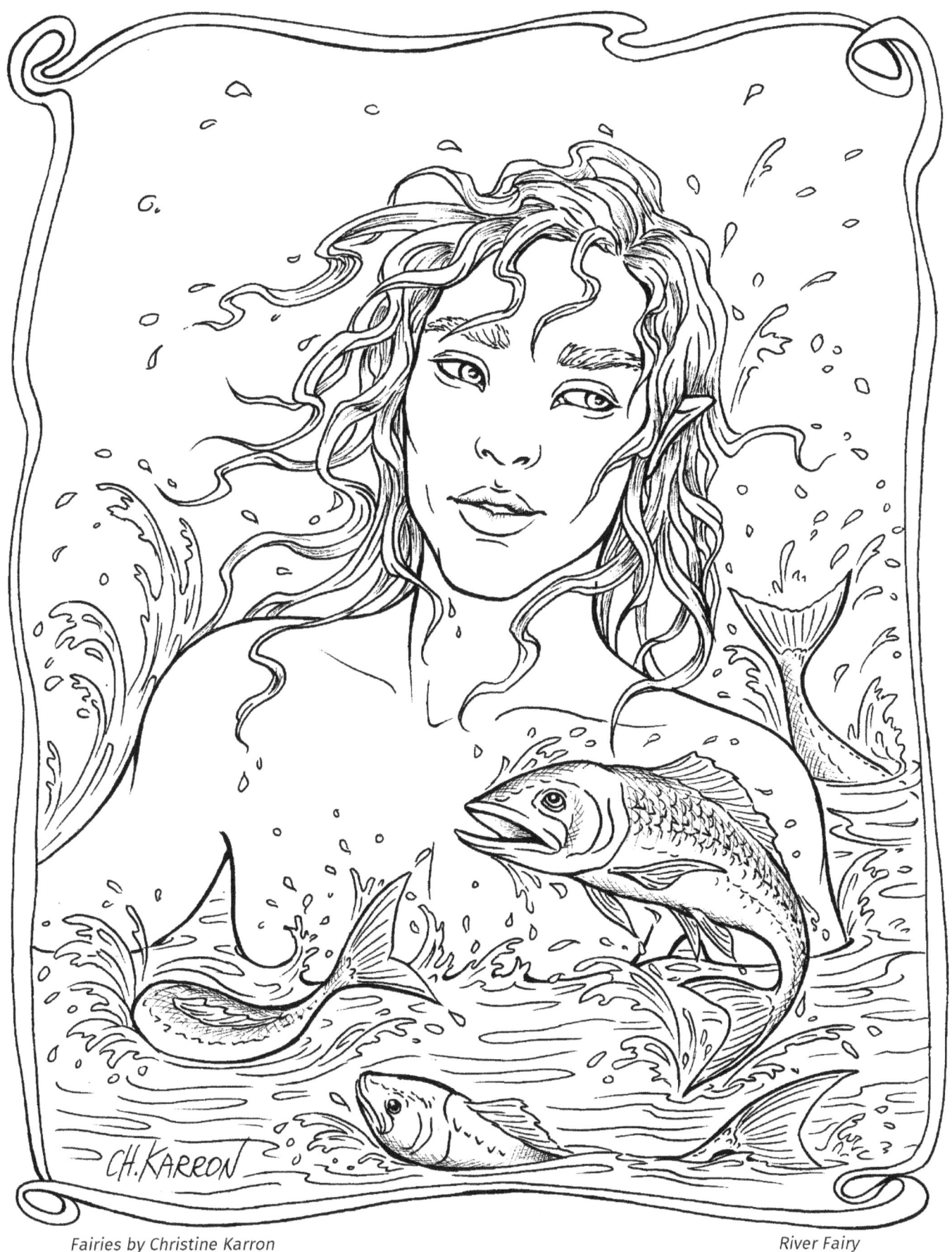

Fairies by Christine Karron

River Fairy

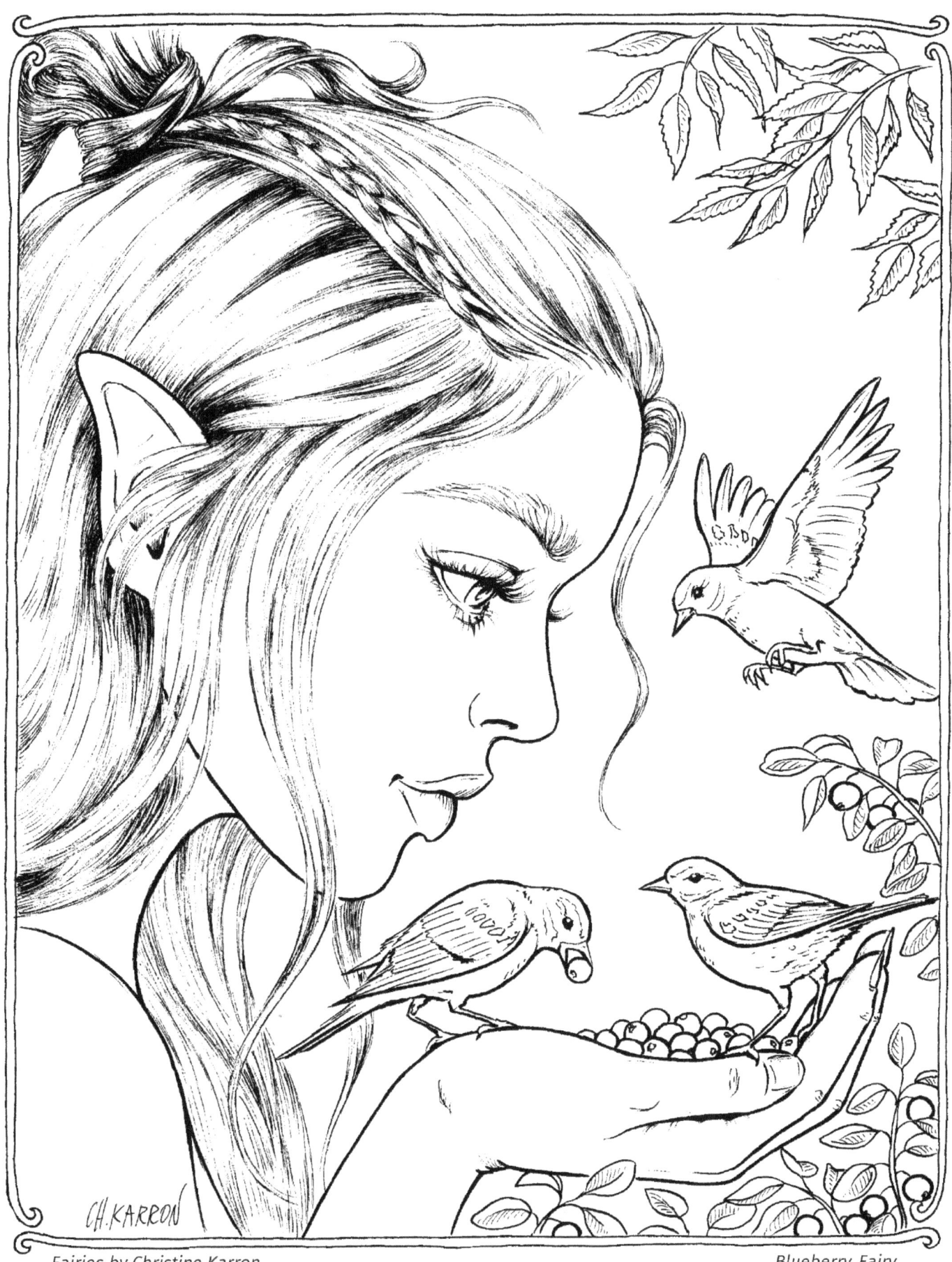

Fairies by Christine Karron

Blueberry Fairy

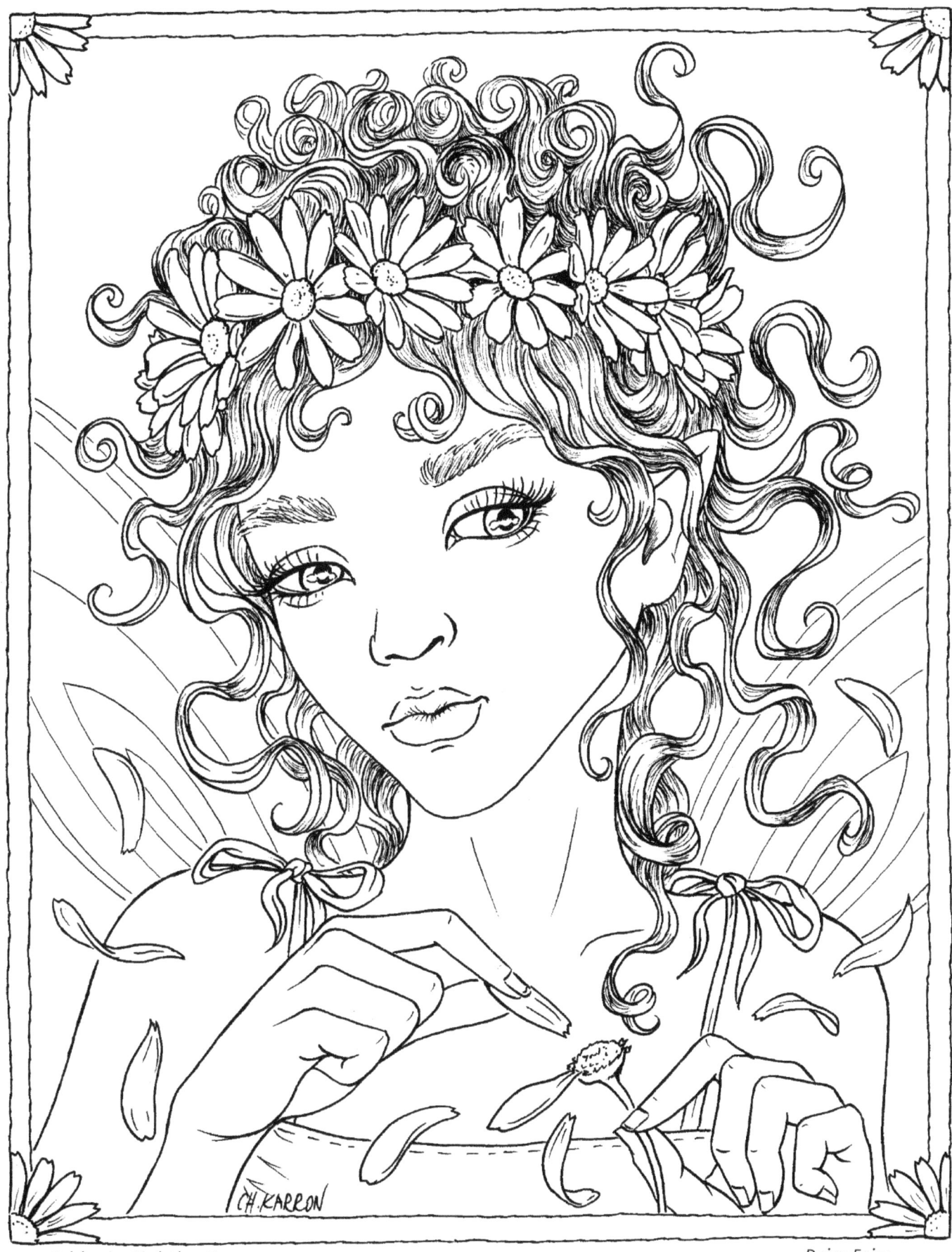

Fairies by Christine Karron

Daisy Fairy

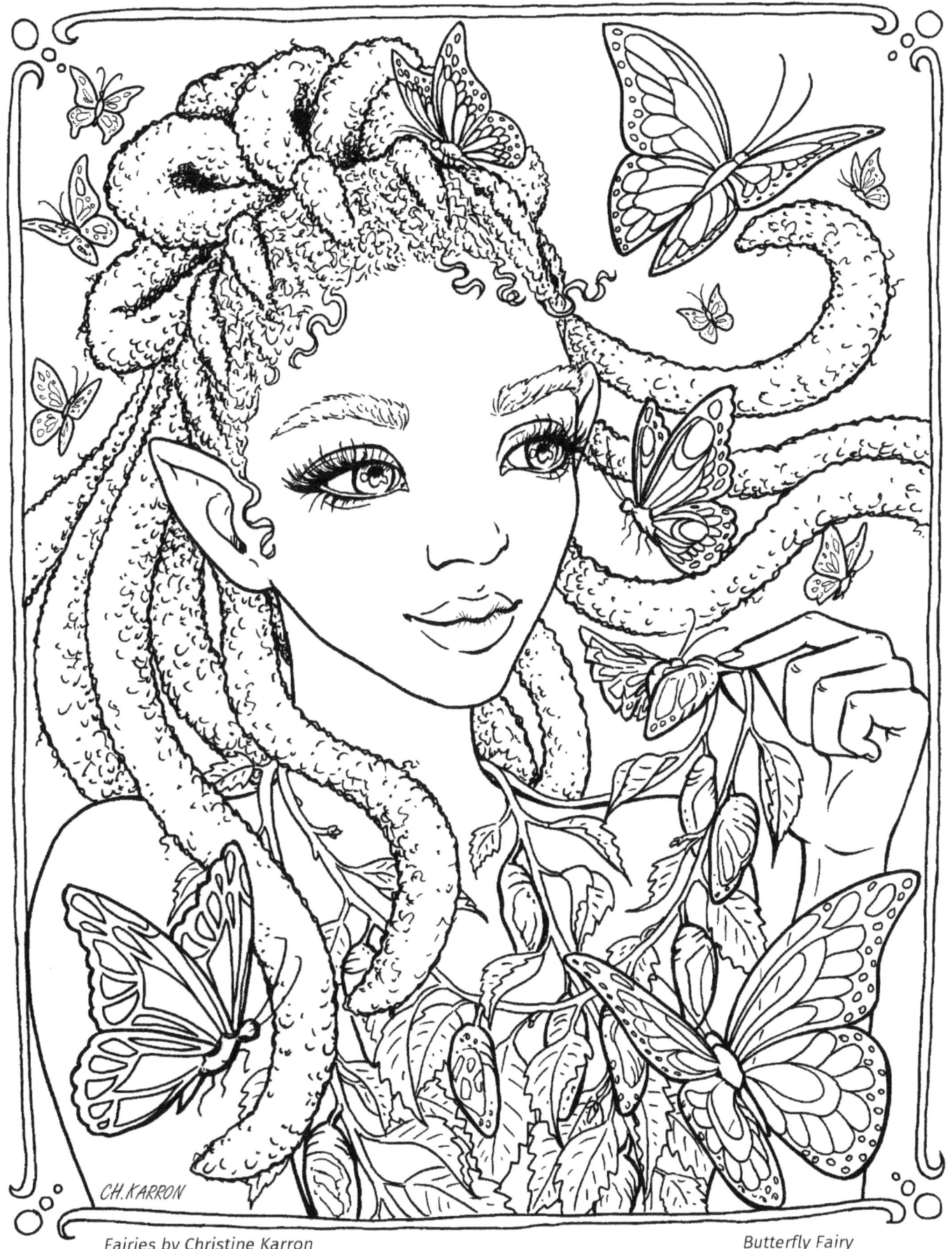

Fairies by Christine Karron

Butterfly Fairy

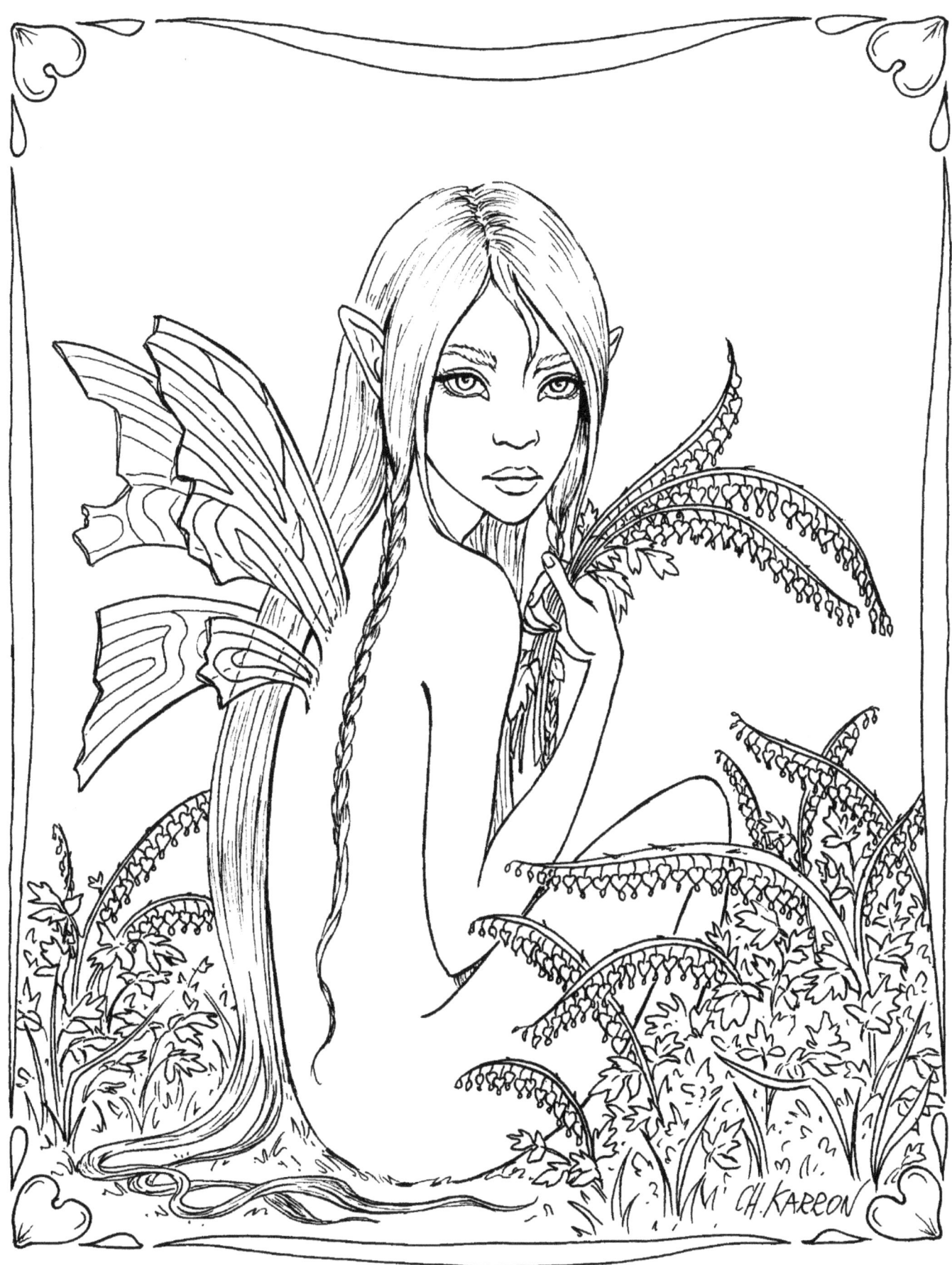

Fairies by Christine Karron   Bleeding Hearts Fairy

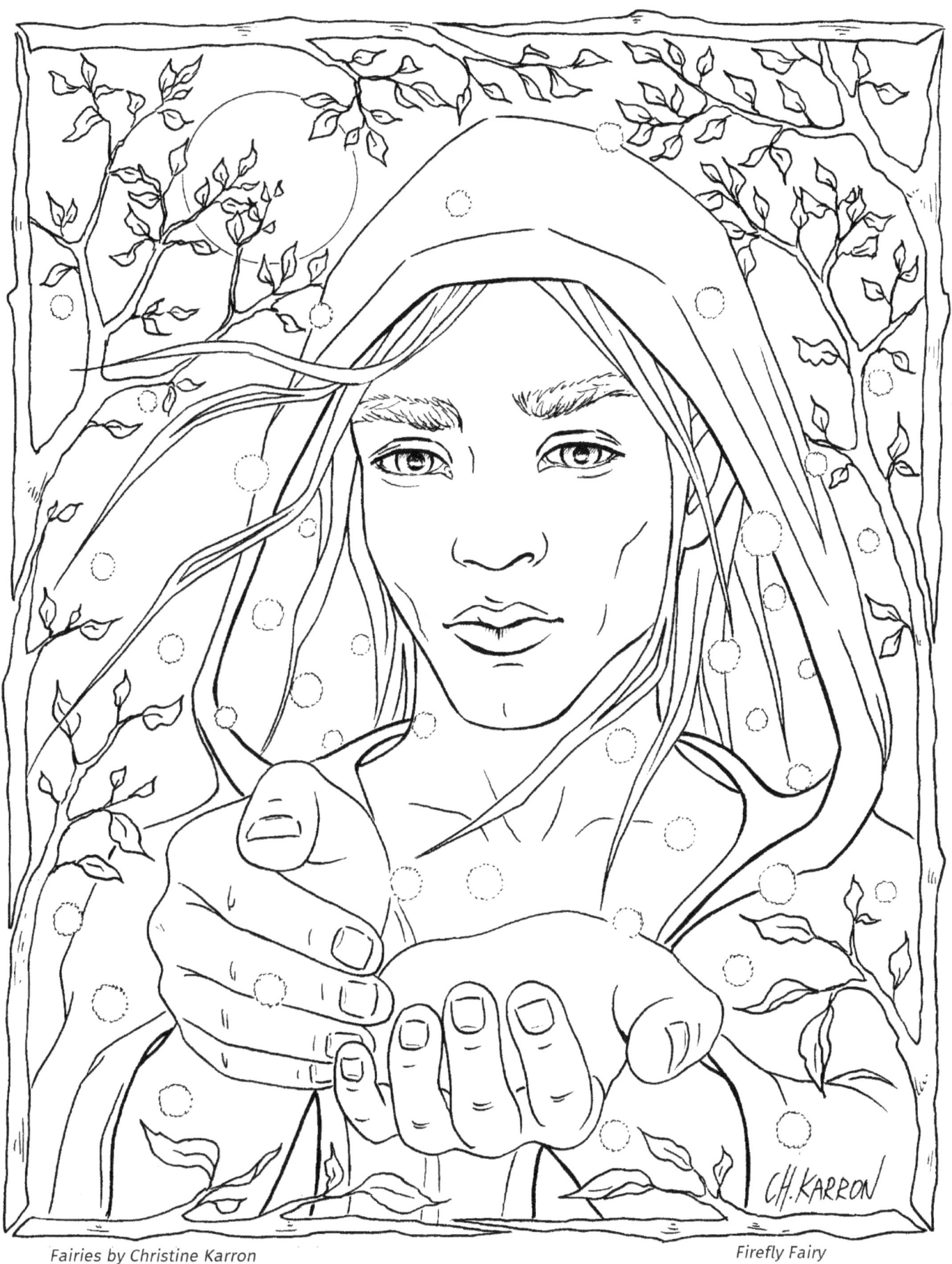

Fairies by Christine Karron

Firefly Fairy

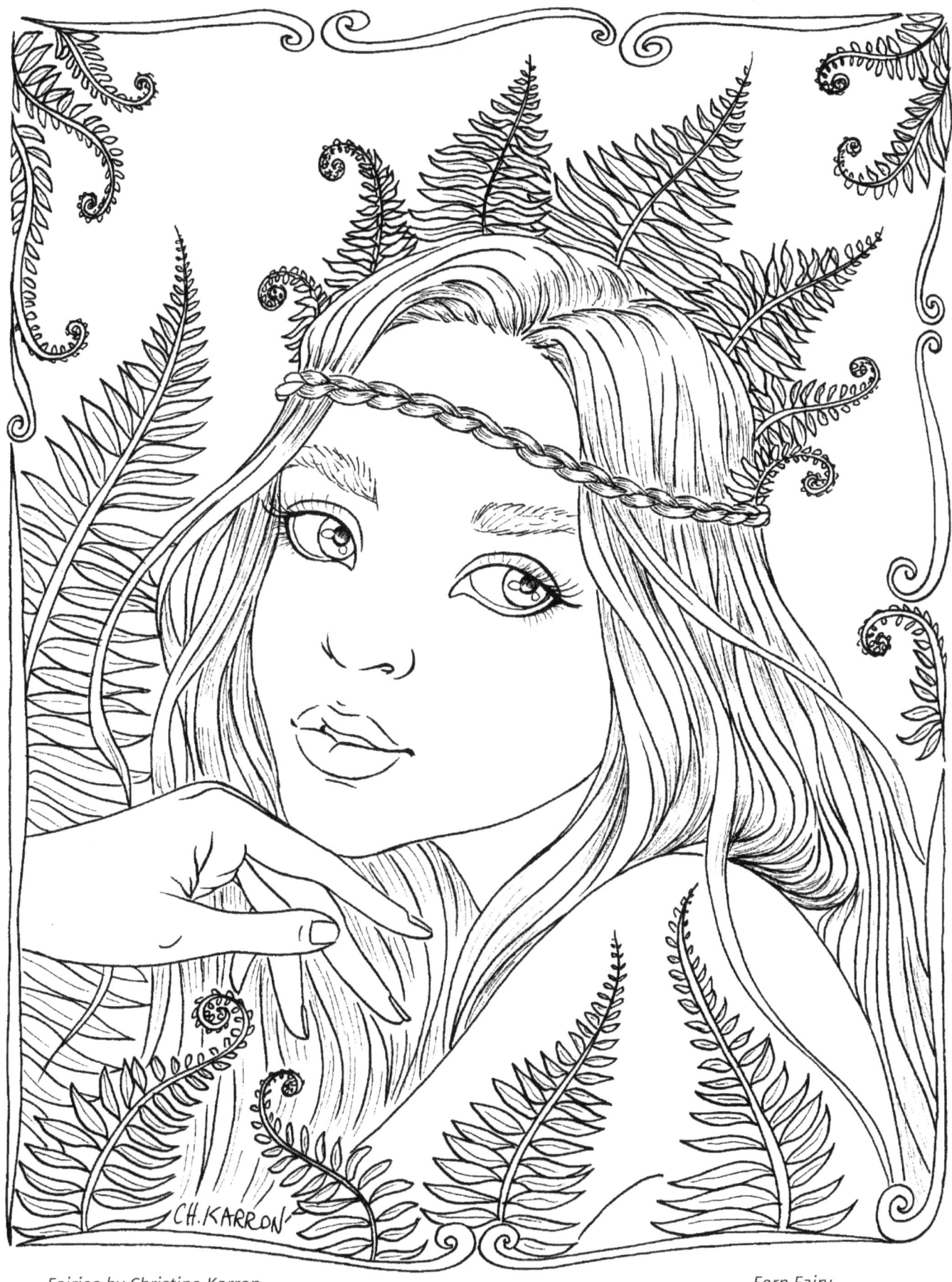

Fairies by Christine Karron

Fern Fairy

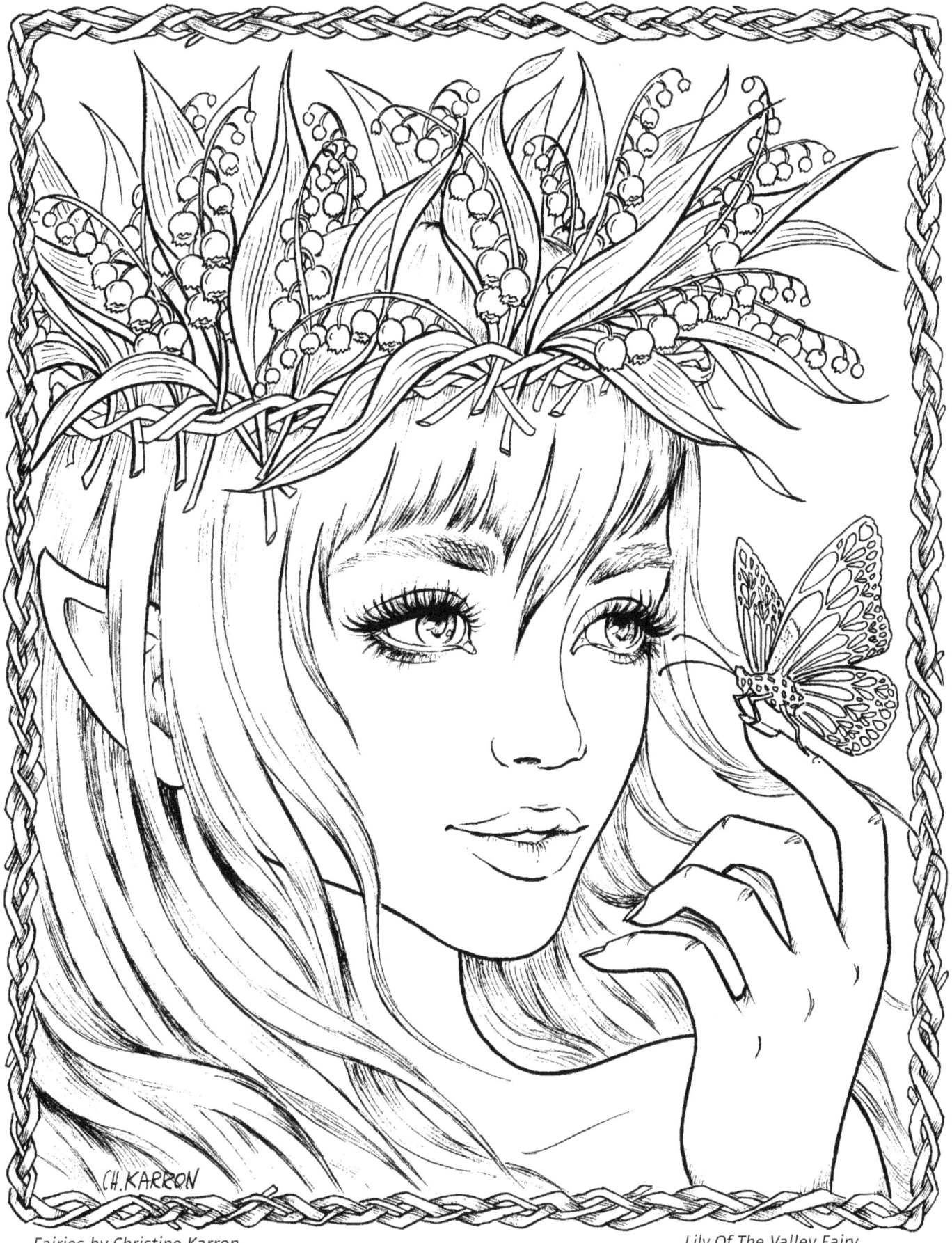

Fairies by Christine Karron

Lily Of The Valley Fairy

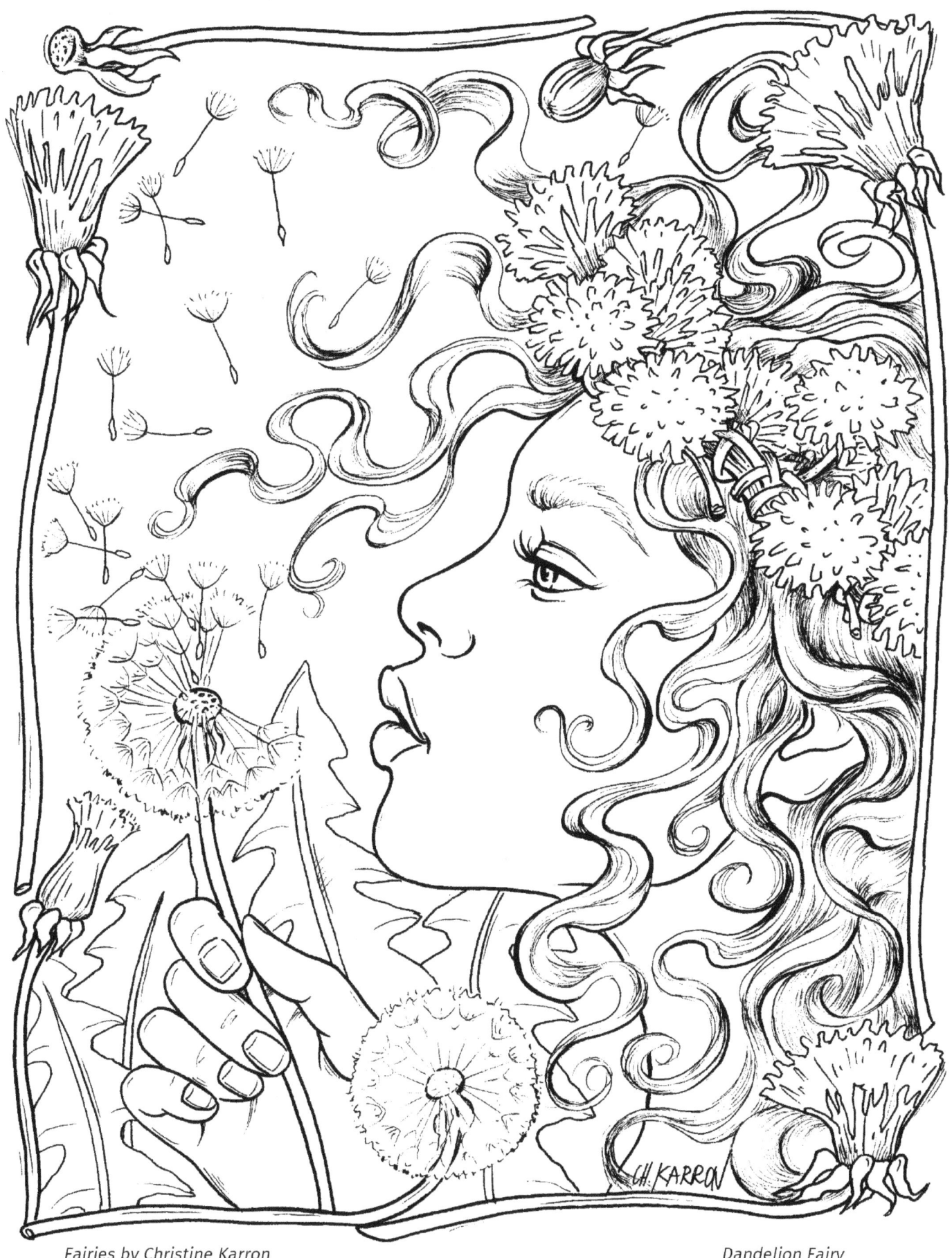

Fairies by Christine Karron

Dandelion Fairy

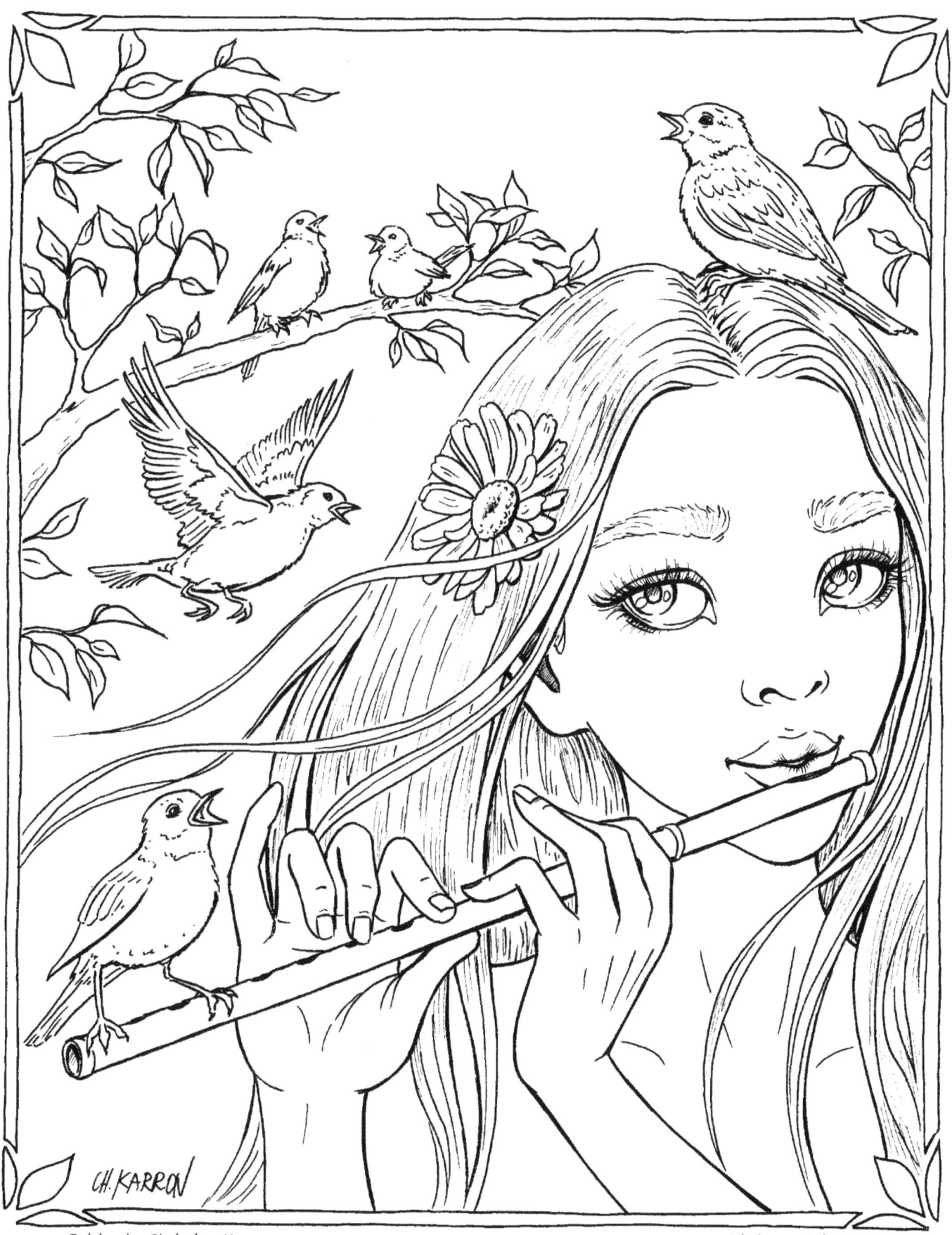

Fairies by Christine Karron

Birdsong Fairy

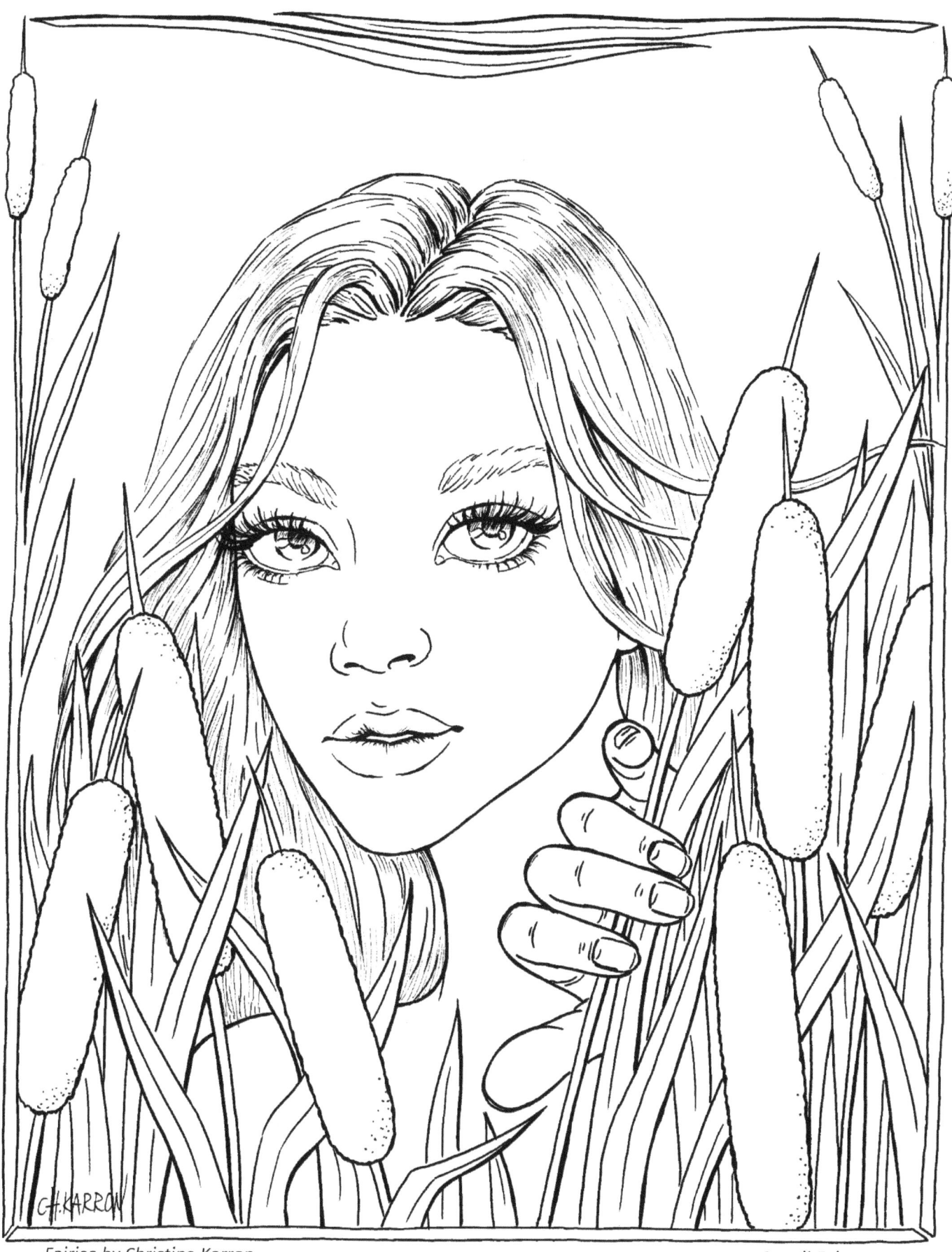

Fairies by Christine Karron

Cattail Fairy

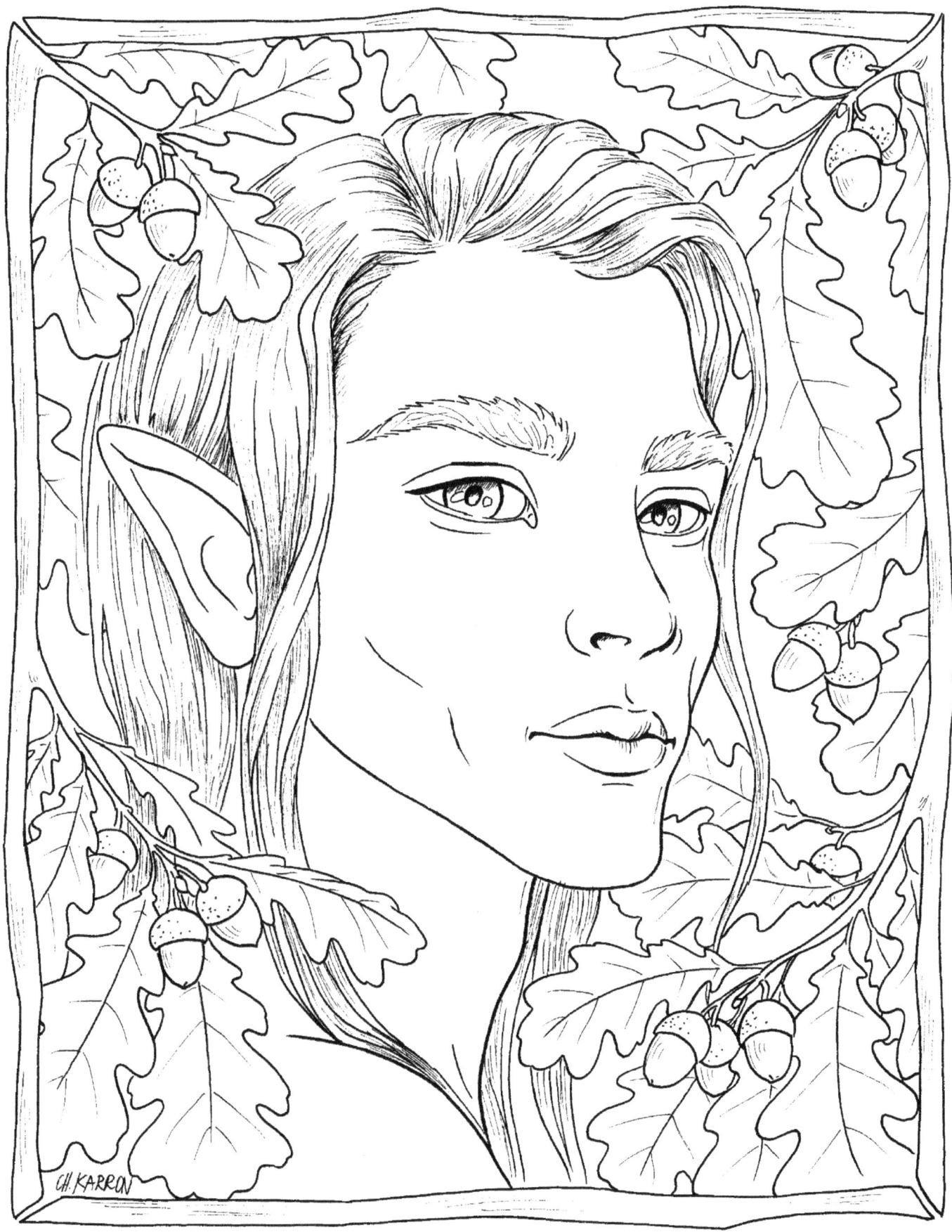

Fairies by Christine Karron

Oak Tree Fairy

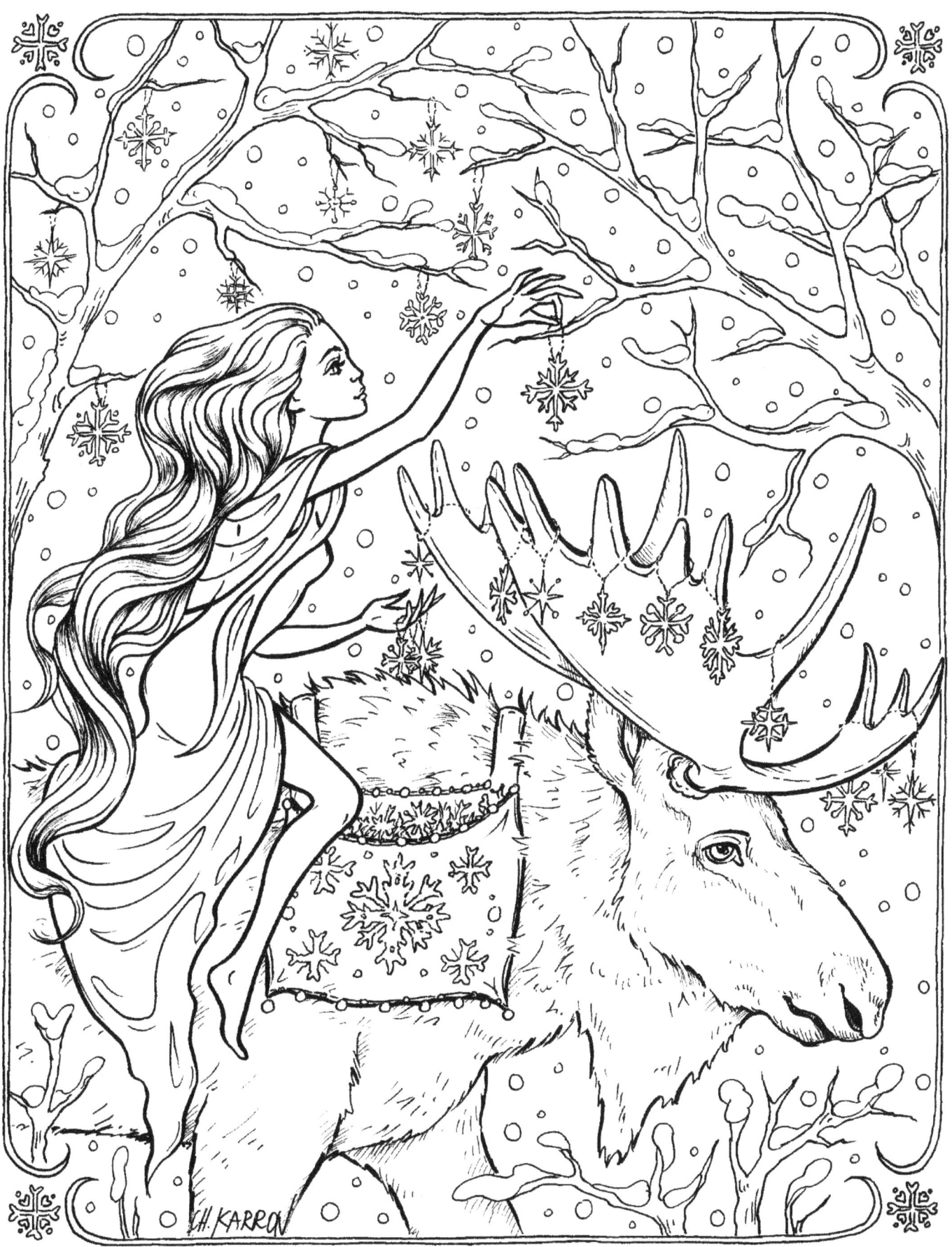

Fairies by Christine Karron

Snow Fairy

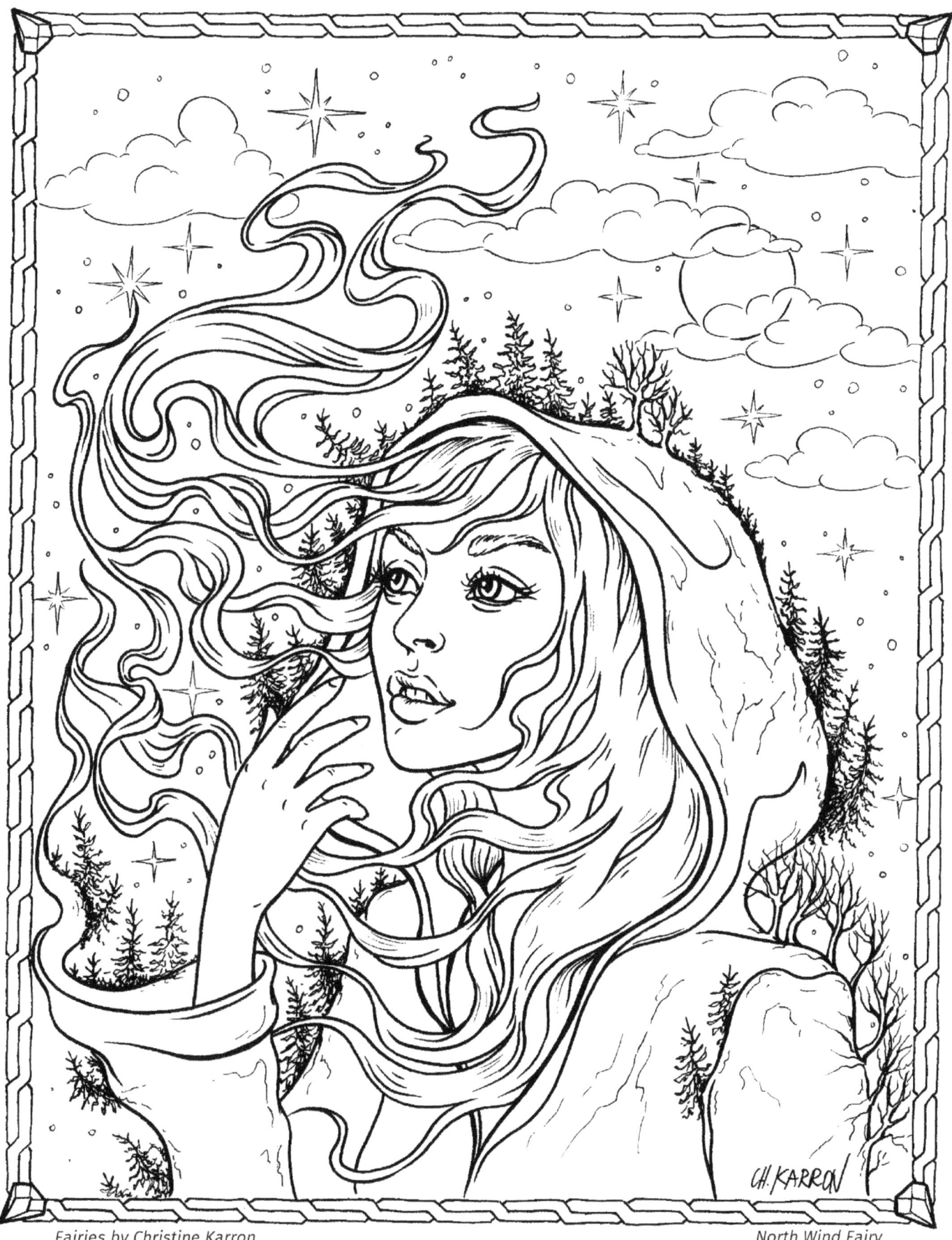

Fairies by Christine Karron

North Wind Fairy

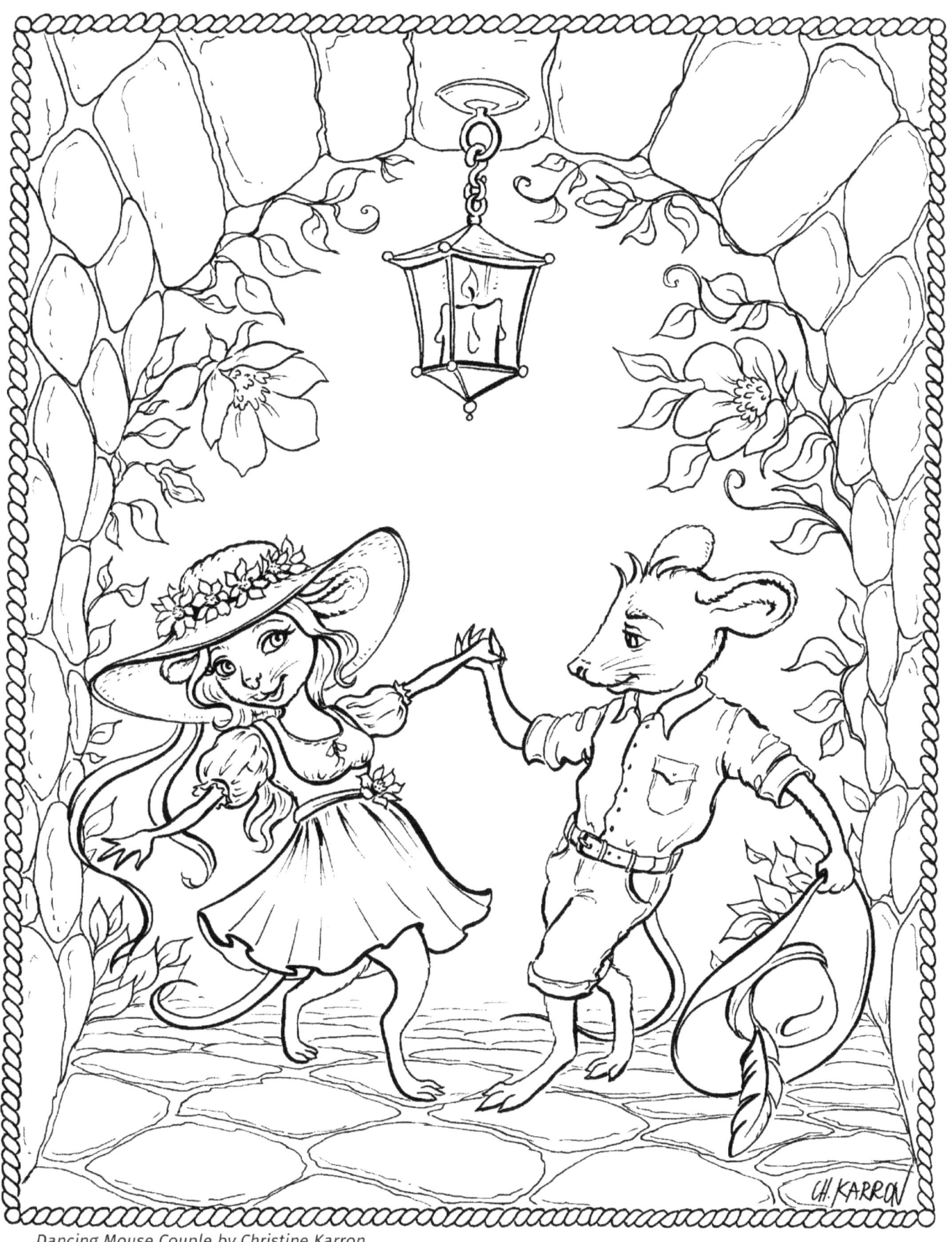
Dancing Mouse Couple by Christine Karron

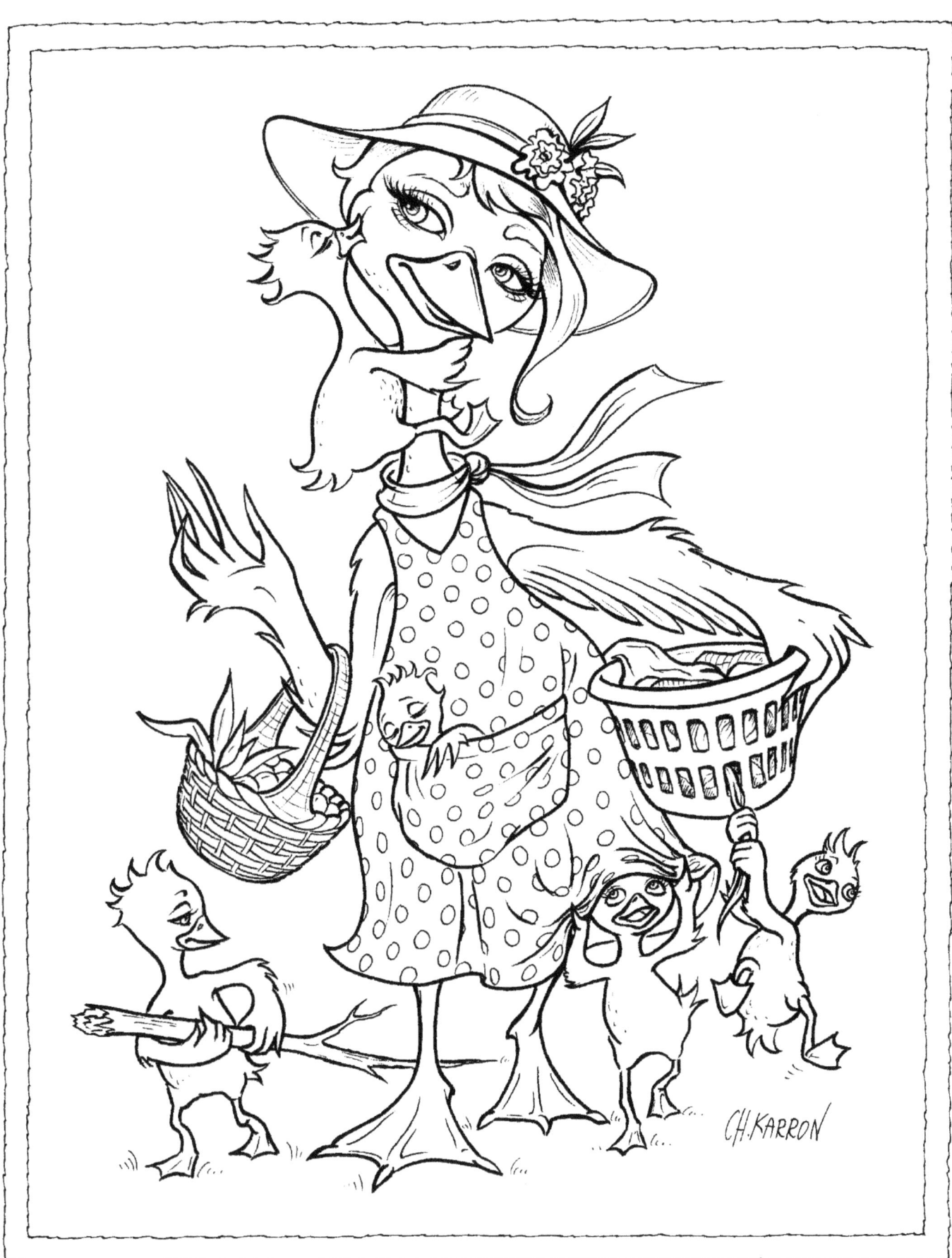

Mother Goose by Christine Karron

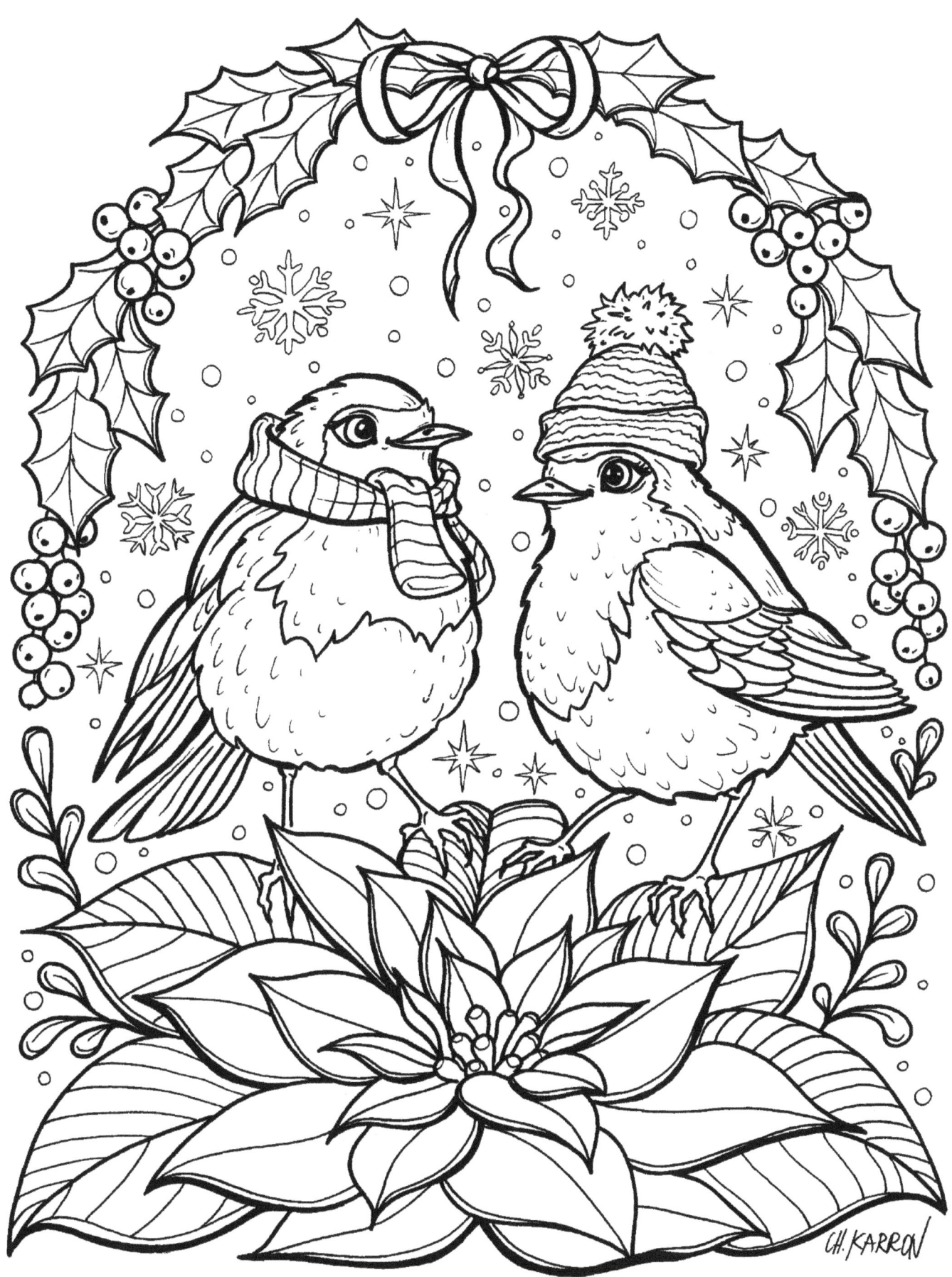

Robin Christmas by Christine Karron

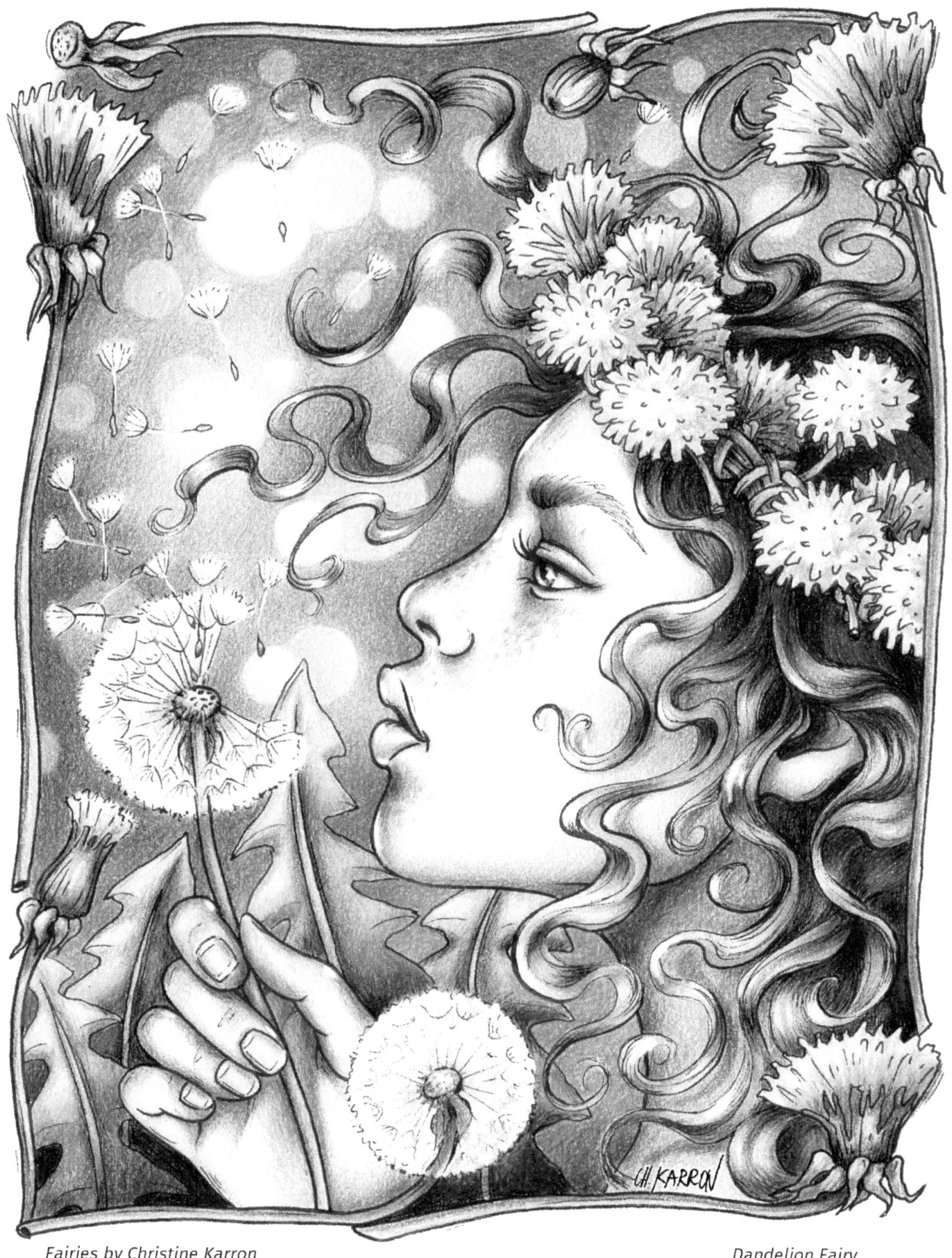

Fairies by Christine Karron

Dandelion Fairy

Christine Karron is a Canadian illustrator and painter.
Originally from Estonia and Germany, Christine has been drawing and painting since she was a small child – she was called an artist before she knew what it meant. With some formal training, self-education and experience, between raising kids and taking care of her family, Christine has been working as a freelance artist for 20 years now. She has exhibited her artwork in numerous shows and sold to clients worldwide. In the last few years, Christine has been focusing more on her passion - children's book illustration and publishing her own books. Christine works and lives with her husband and their three kids in Central Alberta, Canada.

Coloring books by Christine Karron:

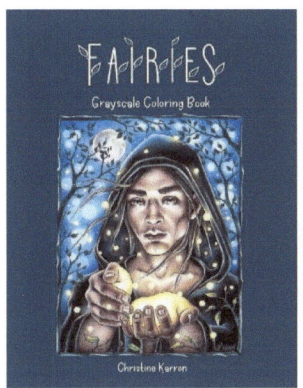 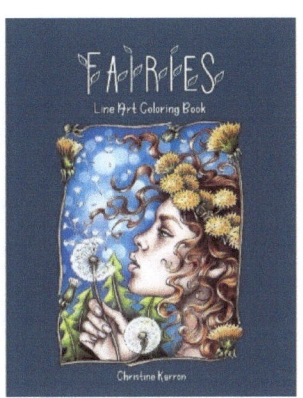 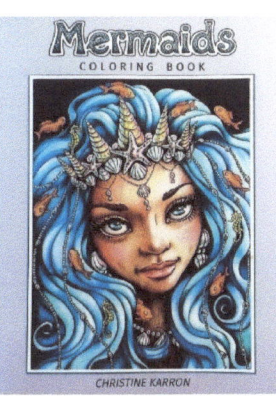 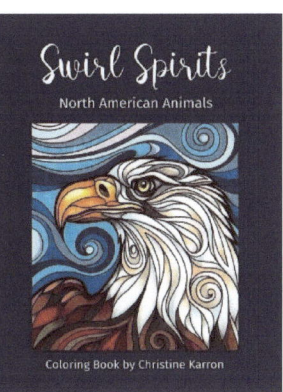

Printable downloads (in PDF format) of Christine Karron's coloring books and coloring pages are available in her Etsy shop Christine Karron.

Visit www.chkarron.com for coloring ideas,
samples and coloring demo videos.

You can follow Christine Karron Art and illustration
on Facebook or Christine Karron on Instagram.

You are welcome to join
Christine Karron Coloring Collection Fan Group on Facebook.

If sharing colored images online please credit the artist - Christine Karron
You can use hashtags #christinekarron and/or #chkarron

Please DO NOT share or post uncolored versions of the images from this book on Facebook, Pinterest or any other sharing sites online.

All rights reserved by Christine Karron.

www.ingramcontent.com/pod-product-compliance
Lightning Source LLC
Chambersburg PA
CBHW051215220526
45473CB00003B/1047